W9-BAZ-626

PROVENANCE EVIDENCE

Thesaurus for Use in
Rare Book and Special Collections Cataloguing

Prepared by the

Standards Committee

of the

Rare Books and Manuscripts Section

(ACRL/ALA)

Chicago

Association of College and Research Libraries

1988

Published by the Association of College and Research Libraries
a division of the American Library Association
50 East Huron Street
Chicago, IL 60611

ISBN 0-8389-7239-X

The paper used in this publication meets the minimum requirements of American National Standard for Information Sciences--Permanence of Paper for Printed Library Materials. ANSI Z39.48-1984. ∞

Copyright © 1988 by the American Library Association. All rights reserved except those which may be granted by Sections 107 and 108 of the Copyright Revision Act of 1976.

Printed in the United States of America.

The Library of Congress has assigned the following USMARC code to this thesaurus:

Provenance terms: rbprov

This code must be entered in subfield $2 of USMARC bibliographic record field 755 when terms from this thesaurus are used in that field. The code in subfield $2 will correspond with the parenthetical qualifier used in subfield $a (see Introduction).

PROVENANCE EVIDENCE

A Thesaurus for Use in Rare Book and Special Collections
Cataloguing

Introduction

I. History

The Independent Research Libraries Association's
Proposals for establishing standards for the cataloguing of
rare books and specialized research materials in machine-
readable form (Worcester, Mass.,1979) called for a new field
to be added to machine-readable cataloging (MARC) formats for
terms indicating the physical characteristics of the
materials catalogued (Proposal 5), including terms relating
to provenance evidence. In the same proposal IRLA requested
that the Standards Committee of the Rare Books and
Manuscripts Section of ACRL work toward developing standard
terminology for use in such a field. The RBMS Standards
Committee undertook the development of a thesaurus of terms,
and a field for such terms (755, "Physical Characteristics
Access") was authorized for all MARC formats in January 1984.

In order to expedite publication of the thesaurus, the
RBMS Standards Committee decided to divide it into several
separate thesauri, each treating evidence of a different
aspect of book production and history. To date the RBMS
Standards Committee has published two thesauri for use in
field 755 for special collections cataloguing: Printing &
Publishing Evidence (Chicago: ACRL, 1986) and Binding
Evidence (Chicago: ACRL, 1988). The Committee is currently
reviewing drafts of similar thesauri for paper and type
evidence. The present list contains terms relating to
evidence for provenance of material catalogued (usually
individual copies of books). "Provenance" is here interpreted
in its broadest sense to refer not only to former owners in
the legal sense, but also to any who may have had temporary
custody of the material (such as auction houses or library
borrowers) and have left their mark in some way on it. The
actual names of former owners are not the province of this
planned access, as owners' names can be traced in name added
entry fields combined with the use of relator terms;
cf. Relator Terms for Rare Book, Manuscript, and Special
Collections. 3rd ed. College & Research Libraries News
(Oct., 1987) [or latest edition]. The terms in the thesaurus

come from drafts of the IRLA proposals, some existing lists in rare book libraries, various reference works, and comments on drafts of the lists by individuals at several institutions. Drafts of this thesaurus were prepared by Dianne Chilmonczyk, based on earlier work by John Lancaster.

II. Purpose and Scope

Many rare book libraries, concerned with the study of the book, maintain local files recording examples of various physical characteristics of items found in their collections. These files are used to retrieve books by physical features rather than by intellectual content. Although such files are useful for selection of materials for exhibition, for class demonstration, and for cataloguing comparison, their primary use is to assist researchers interested in studying the physical characteristics of books as evidence of their production, distribution, or further history.

Reflecting for the most part local rather than standard cataloguing practices, such files have usually remained available only within individual libraries. Developed specifically for use in MARC field 755, the following thesaurus provides standard terms for the retrieval of provenance evidence. Such standardization is a necessity for those institutions working in the context of shared, machine-readable cataloguing but may also prove beneficial to those maintaining in-house files.

III. Form

This thesaurus consists of an alphabetical list of terms, followed by an hierarchical display. Following ANSI standards (American National Standards Institute, American National Guidelines for Thesaurus Construction and Use, New York, 1980), the terms are in plural natural language noun form whenever possible, and in direct order. Adjectives and prepositions have been avoided as far as possible. An attempt has been made to include both genus (e.g., "Bookplates") and species (e.g., "Armorial bookplates") terms in a number of cases.

Terms of the form "[adjective] copies" are of a slightly different nature from other terms in this list, in that they denote, not a type of evidence, but a condition of association. They were developed in response to three considerations: 1) that a need was felt for terms indicating connections with certain classes of owners commonly involved with books (e.g., Authors' copies, Dedicatees' copies etc.) and 2) that a need was felt for terms indicating the occasion for the provenance or method of acquisition (e.g., Presentation copies), but 3) that to provide a range of more specific terms for each class of owners or each occasion of provenance, combined with each type of physical evidence, would lead to an unwieldy proliferation of terms (e.g., Authors' armorial presentation bindings, Illustrators' edge-marks, etc.) not to mention incomplete coverage.

The alphabetical list contains authorized terms and appropriate cross references. Scope notes follow terms thought to be obscure or ambiguous, or which are to be used in a technical sense. Each term is followed by the references, if any, made to and from other terms in the thesaurus. Symbols used in these references are those which ANSI prescribes:

> USE leads from unused synonyms and inverted forms of the term to the term used;
>
> UF (used for) is the reciprocal of the USE reference and accompanies the term to which the USE reference refers;
>
> BT (broader term) refers from a term for a member of a class to the term for the class;
>
> NT (narrower term) refers from a term for a class to the term for one of its members;
>
> RT (related term) is used between related terms when it seems helpful to bring associated types of evidence to the user's attention.

In the present thesaurus, members of a class related to each other as narrower terms (NTs) under a common class (BT) are not referenced to each other as related terms (RT). However, whenever a term for which there are narrower terms in the thesaurus appears under another term as either a narrower term (NT) or a related term (RT), it is followed by the symbol ">" to indicate that it is not the narrowest concept of its class. Users should consult the entry in the alphabetical list for terms so marked to identify narrower terms.

The separate hierarchical list (see pp. 18-19) of provenance terms is furnished to provide a convenient overview. The hierarchical display shows no cross references. The hierarchy contains several explanatory or gathering terms (displayed within square brackets). These terms are not authorized for use in field 755 and do not appear in the alphabetical list.

IV. Application

In a MARC record, these terms are to be entered in subfield $a ("access term") of field 755. Terms which do not appear in this or other thesauri approved for field 755 may not be used in this field. When used in a MARC record, a parenthetical qualifier must be added in subfield $a following the term. The qualifier will aid users who may not see or know how to interpret coding for subfield $2 (see below), and it also helps clarify terms which are ambiguous when taken out of context (e.g., "Devices"). Terms from the present list receive the qualifier "(Provenance)".

Any term in this thesaurus may be subdivided by place ($z), period ($y), or other subdivision ($x), or by any combination of these subdivisions. Each library must determine its own scheme for chronological subdivision. Indirect subdivision, as outlined in LC's Cataloging Service Bulletin 120 (1977), pp. 9-11, is to be used when subdividing by place. Libraries using other subdivisions ($x) should construct these subdivisions to conform as much as possible to LC practice as defined in publications such as Library of Congress Subject Headings: A Guide to Subdivision Practice (Washington, 1981) or Cataloging Service Bulletin.

Each 755 field must close with a subfield $2 ("source of access term"). The Library of Congress has assigned the code "rbprov" to this thesaurus. Therefore, 755 fields using terms from this list must close with $2 "rbprov".

An example of the application of a subdivided term:

755 ƀƀ $aBookplates (Provenance)$zGermany$y18th century.$2rbprov

N.B. : Subfields $a (with qualifier) and $2 are mandatory; other subfields are optional.

Field 755 is repeatable; assign as many terms as appropriate and desired to retrieve types of evidence in an item. For example, a book having an author's presentation inscription, a bookplate, and a monogrammed binding might have three 755 entries, one for each term.

Use of field 755 is voluntary. Some libraries may want to use the field only for several of the terms; other libraries may prefer to use none. In the case of those terms linked by a genus-species relationship, some libraries may wish to use only the broader term; other libraries may prefer to assign only the narrower terms when appropriate, reserving the broader terms for items not covered by any narrower terms in the thesaurus.

The thesaurus of provenance terms is designed to create special files in a library of any size, whether it has only a few unusual items that might be identified for teaching or exhibition purposes, or a large collection in which particular characteristics are kept track of systematically. A small file is more likely to consist of general terms, while a large one will probably contain many more specific terms, but these decisions must be based on the institution's needs.

Provenance terms and evidence are usually copy-specific. Libraries doing original cataloguing should describe as desired the characteristics of their own copies; other libraries making later use of such cataloguing will probably need to delete the 755 provenance entries.

These terms are to be used in field 755 regardless of the appearance of the same information elsewhere in the record (such as in a subject heading or in a note), their primary purpose being to provide easy retrieval of examples of provenance evidence through a single source.

The following works may prove helpful to persons needing fuller descriptions of some of the types of evidence represented by terms in the thesaurus:

ALA Glossary of Library and Information Science. Chicago : ALA, 1983.

Carter, John. ABC for Book-Collectors. London ; New York : Granada, 1980 (or latest edition).

Glaister, G.A. Glaister's Glossary of the Book. 2nd. ed. Berkeley : University of California Press, 1979.

Harrod, L.M. Librarians' Glossary. Aldershot, Hants ; Brookfield, Vt., U.S.A. : Gower, 1984.

Stoddard, Roger E. Marks in Books, Illustrated and Explained. Cambridge, Mass.: Houghton Library, Harvard University, 1985.

V. Revision

The RBMS Standards Committee is responsible for the maintenance and revision of these thesauri. It solicits suggestions for new terms, corrections, and alterations to terms, scope notes and references. Any new term proposed should be accompanied by a scope note and references if appropriate. Any correspondence regarding this thesaurus should be addressed to:

Chair, Standards Committee
Rare Books and Manuscripts Section
ACRL/ALA
50 East Huron Street
Chicago, Il 60611

Attention: Provenance Evidence

RBMS Standards Committee Members, 1986-1987

Dianne M. Chilmonczyk	Sara Shatford Layne
Michele Cloonan	Hope Mayo
Alan N. Degutis	Elisabeth Betz Parker
Jackie M. Dooley	Joe Springer
Rebecca Hayne	John B. Thomas III

PROVENANCE EVIDENCE

Thesaurus for Use in Rare Book and Special Collections
Cataloguing

I. Alphabetical list

Accession numbers
    BT Numbers
    RT Library copies

Annotations
    (Use for remarks, notes, highlighting or commentary
    (generally in manuscript) on the text or on the history or
    provenance of the material.)
    BT Markings
    NT Authors' annotations
        Dates >
        Fists
        Genealogical notes
        Marginalia
        Prices
        Underscoring

Armorial bindings
    BT Bindings
    RT Armorial stamps
        Devices

Armorial bookplates
    UF Heraldic bookplates
    BT Bookplates
    RT Armorial stamps
        Devices

Armorial stamps
    BT Stamps
    RT Armorial bindings
        Armorial bookplates
        Devices

Association copies
    (Use for evidence of association when a broad scope is
    desired. This could include copies of books owned or
    annotated by the author, someone connected with the author,
    someone of interest in his own right, or someone
    particularly associated with the contents or production of
    the book. Some institutions may choose to further broaden
    the scope of this term by including indeterminate evidence
    of association.)
    NT Authors' copies
       Booksellers' copies
       Dedicatees' copies
       Donors' copies
       Illustrators' copies
       Library copies
       Printers' copies
       Publishers' copies
    RT False association copies
       Illegible markings
       Supposed association copies

Association copies, False
    USE False association copies

Association copies, Supposed
    USE Supposed associated copies

Auction copies
    (Use for copies known to have been sold at auction.)
    RT Auction lot numbers

Auction lot numbers
    BT Numbers
    RT Auction copies

Authors' annotations
    BT Annotations
    RT Authors' copies

Authors' autographs
    BT Autographs
    RT Authors' copies

Authors' copies
  (Use for copies of an author's work known or thought to
  have been part of that author's personal library or used by
  that author, not simply presented or inscribed by the
  author.)
  BT Association copies
  RT Authors' annotations
     Authors' autographs
     Authors' inscriptions >
     Authors' presentation copies

Authors' inscriptions
  BT Inscriptions
  NT Authors' presentation inscriptions
  RT Authors' copies

Authors' presentation copies
  BT Presentation copies
  RT Authors' copies
     Authors' presentation inscriptions

Authors' presentation inscriptions
  BT Authors' inscriptions
     Presentation inscriptions
  RT Authors' presentation copies

Autographs
  UF Signatures
  BT Markings
  NT Authors' autographs
  RT Initials combined with printed signatures

Award books
  USE Prize books

Binders' tickets
  BT Labels
  RT Bindings >

Bindings
  (Use for bindings with some characteristic that might allow
  identification of the provenance, whether or not the
  provenance is actually identified.)
  NT Armorial bindings
     Branded bindings
     Dedication bindings
     Monogrammed bindings
     Presentation bindings
  RT Binders' tickets

Blind stamps
    BT Stamps

Booklabels
    USE Bookplates

Bookplates
    UF Booklabels
    BT Labels
    NT Armorial bookplates
        Donors' bookplates

Booksellers' copies
    (Use for copies owned by booksellers or displaying evidence
    of second-hand booksales, *e.g.*, dealer's ms. notes.)
    BT Association copies
    RT Booksellers' labels

Booksellers' labels
    UF Stationers' labels
    BT Labels
    RT Booksellers' copies

Branded bindings
    BT Bindings
    RT Branded edges

Branded edges
    BT Edge-marks
    RT Branded bindings

Call numbers
    USE Shelf marks

Cancellation stamps
    USE Release stamps

Ciphers (Codes)
    USE Codes

Ciphers (Monograms)
    USE Monograms

Codes
    (Use for booksellers' or owners' codes, ciphers, price
    codes.)
    UF Ciphers (Codes)
    BT Markings
    RT Booksellers' copies

Dates
    (Use for evidence dating the acquisition or period of
    ownership.)
    BT Annotations
    NT Reading dates

Dedicatees' copies
    BT Association copies

Dedication bindings
    BT Bindings
    RT Presentation bindings

Devices
    (Use for evidence of any physical form which uses a family
    or personal emblem.)
    UF Emblems
    BT Markings
    RT Armorial bindings
       Armorial bookplates
       Armorial stamps

Donors' copies
    (Use for materials actually owned and then donated by an
    individual or institution.)
    BT Association copies
    RT Donors' bookplates

Donors' bookplates
    BT Bookplates
    RT Donors' copies

Duplicate stamps
    BT Release stamps

Edge-marks
    BT Markings
    NT Branded edges

Emblems
    USE Devices

Embossed stamps
    BT Stamps

Extra-illustrated copies
    UF Grangerized copies
    BT Insertions

False association copies
(Use for forged, faked or discredited evidence of
provenance, usually in conjunction with another term or
terms from this list.)
UF Association copies, False
RT Association copies >
Supposed association copies

Family trees
USE Genealogical notes

Fists
(Use for previous owners' indications drawing attention to
text.)
UF Index fingers
Note signs
Pointing hands
BT Annotations

Genealogical notes
UF Family trees
BT Annotatiions

Grangerized copies
USE Extra-illustrated copies

Hand stamps
USE Stamps

Heraldic bookplates
USE Armorial bookplates

Illegible markings
BT Markings
RT Association copies >
Supposed association copies

Illustrators' copies
BT Association copies

Index fingers
USE Fists

Initials
BT Markings
NT Initials combined with printed signatures
Stencilled initials

Initials combined with printed signatures
  (Use for evidence of provenance consisting of a combination
  of manuscript initials and printed signature marks, _e.g._,
  Thomas Jefferson's additions of the letter "T" preceding
  signature mark "I" or "J" following signature mark "T".)
  BT Initials
  RT Autographs >

Ink stamps
  BT Stamps

Inscriptions
  BT Markings
  NT Authors' inscriptions >
     Presentation inscriptions >

Insertions
  (Use for any kind of insertion that might allow
  identification of the provenance, _e.g._, autograph letter,
  news clipping, photograph, etc.)
  NT Extra-illustrated copies
     Presentation insertions >
  RT Markings >

Labels
  (Use for evidence of provenance applied by adhesion rather
  than impression.)
  NT Binders' tickets
     Bookplates >
     Booksellers' labels
  RT Markings >

Library copies
  (Use for copies owned by institutions or formal private
  libraries as opposed to personal collections.)
  BT Association copies
  RT Accession numbers
     Shelf marks
     Withdrawn copies

Marginalia
  BT Annotations

Markings
  (Use for any distinctive feature impressed manually or mechanically on materials to designate provenance.)
  NT Annotations >
     Autographs >
     Codes
     Devices
     Edge-marks >
     Illegible markings
     Initials >
     Inscriptions >
     Monograms >
     Mottoes
     Numbers >
     Seals
     Shelf marks
     Stamps >
     Stencils
     Watermarks
  RT Bindings >
     Insertions >
     Labels >
     Papers >

Monogrammed bindings
  BT Bindings

Monograms
  UF Ciphers (Monograms)
  BT Markings
  NT Stencilled monograms

Mottoes
  BT Markings

Note signs
  USE Fists

Numbers
  (Use for marks of provenance which use numerical designations with or without other codes.)
  BT Markings
  NT Accession numbers
     Auction lot numbers

Papers
   (Use for paper evidence indicating that individual
   printers, publishers, collectors or owners had their own
   papers made with identifying fibers or watermarks for their
   own copies.)
   NT Paper fibers
      Watermarks
   RT Markings >

Paper fibers
   BT Papers

Perforation stamps
   BT Stamps

Pointing hands
   USE Fists

Presentation bindings
   BT Bindings
   RT Dedication bindings
      Presentation inscriptions >
      Presentation insertions >
      Prize books

Presentation copies
   NT Authors' presentation copies

Presentation inscriptions
   BT Inscriptions
   NT Authors' presentation inscriptions
   RT Presentation bindings
      Presentation insertions >

Presentation insertions
   BT Insertions
   NT Presentation leaves
   RT Presentation bindings
      Presentation inscriptions >

Presentation leaves
   BT Presentation insertions

Pressmarks
   USE Shelf marks

Prices
   (Use for prices in materials indicating purchase cost
   information by a previous owner or relating to secondary
   selling, _e.g._, second-hand dealer prices, auction prices.)
   BT Annotations>

Printers' copies
   BT Association copies

Prize books
   UF Award books
   RT Presentation bindings

Publishers' copies
   BT Association copies

Reading dates
   BT Dates

Release stamps
   UF Cancellation stamps
      Withdrawal stamps
   BT Stamps
   NT Duplicate stamps
   RT Withdrawn copies

Rubber stamps
   USE Stamps

Seals
   BT Markings

Shelf marks
   UF Call numbers
      Pressmarks
   BT Markings
   RT Library copies

Signatures
   USE Autographs

Stamps
  (Use for evidence left by any mechanical device used to
  create a mark of ownership.)
  UF Hand stamps
     Rubber stamps
  BT Markings
  NT Armorial stamps
     Blind stamps
     Embossed stamps
     Ink stamps
     Perforation stamps
     Release stamps

Stationers' labels
  USE Booksellers' labels

Stencils
  BT Markings
  RT Stencilled initials
     Stencilled monograms

Stencilled initials
  BT Initials
  RT Stencils

Stencilled monograms
  BT Monograms
  RT Stencils

Supposed association copies
  UF Association copies, Supposed
  RT Association copies >
     Illegible markings
     False association copies

Underscoring
  BT Annotations

Watermarks
  BT Markings
     Papers

Withdrawal stamps
  USE Release stamps

Withdrawn copies
  (Use for evidence indicating institutional withdrawal of
  materials.)
  RT Library copies

II: Hierarchical list of terms relating to provenance
    The arrangement of terms in this list is by broad
functional classification, with subclassifications within
larger categories. A term which is applicable to more than
one general category may occur in each. Certain terms (shown
within square brackets [ ]) have been supplied only as
explanatory or gathering terms and are not authorized for use
in MARC field 755; all other terms in this list are direct
entry terms which will be found also in the alphabetical list
(section I).

[Classes of owners]
    Association copies
        Authors' copies
        Booksellers' copies
        Dedicatees' copies
        Donors' copies
        Illustrators' copies
        Library copies
        Printers' copies
        Publishers' copies
    False association copies
    Supposed association copies

[Occasions of provenance]
    Auction copies
    Presentation copies
        Authors' presentation copies
    Prize books
    Withdrawn copies

[Physical amendments]
    Bindings
        Armorial bindings
        Branded bindings
        Dedication bindings
        Monogrammed bindings
        Presentation bindings
    Insertions
        Extra-illustrated copies
        Presentation insertions
            Presentation leaves
    Labels
        Binders' tickets
        Bookplates
            Armorial bookplates
            Donors' bookplates
        Booksellers' labels

Markings
  Annotations
    Authors' annotations
    Dates
      Reading dates
    Fists
    Genealogical notes
    Marginalia
    Prices
    Underscoring
  Autographs
    Authors' autographs
  Codes
  Devices
  Edge-marks
    Branded edges
  Emblems
  Illegible markings
  Initials
    Initials combined with printed signatures
    Stencilled initials
  Inscriptions
    Authors' inscriptions
      Authors' presentation inscriptions
    Presentation inscriptions
      Authors' presentation inscriptions
  Monograms
    Stencilled monograms
  Mottoes
  Numbers
    Accession numbers
    Auction lot numbers
  Prices
  Seals
  Shelf marks
  Stamps
    Armorial stamps
    Blind stamps
    Embossed stamps
    Ink stamps
    Perforation stamps
    Release stamps
      Duplicate stamps
  Stencils
  Watermarks
Papers
  Paper fibers
  Watermarks